THE REAL SCIENCE OF
TIME TRAVEL

Corey Anderson

Lerner Publications ◆ Minneapolis

Lerner Publications Company
An imprint of Lerner Publishing Group, Inc.
241 First Avenue North
Minneapolis, MN 55401 USA

For reading levels and more information, look up this title at www.lernerbooks.com.

Library of Congress Cataloging-in-Publication Data

Names: Anderson, Corey, author.
Title: The real science of time travel / Corey Anderson.
Description: Minneapolis : Lerner Publications, [2022] | Series: The real science of superpowers (Alternator books) | Includes bibliographical references and index. | Audience: Ages 8–12 | Audience: Grades 4–6 | Summary: "In human experience, time travel has always been the subject of fantasy stories. But as scientists learn more about people and the universe, they're starting to realize that some forms of time travel might be possible"— Provided by publisher.
Identifiers: LCCN 2021021287 (print) | LCCN 2021021288 (ebook) | ISBN 9781728441245 (library binding) | ISBN 9781728449609 (paperback) | ISBN 9781728445335 (ebook)
Subjects: LCSH: Time travel—Juvenile literature. | Space and time—Juvenile literature. | Superheroes—Juvenile literature.
Classification: LCC QB209.5 .A53 2022 (print) | LCC QB209.5 (ebook) | DDC 530.11—dc23

LC record available at https://lccn.loc.gov/2021021287
LC ebook record available at https://lccn.loc.gov/2021021288

Manufactured in the United States of America
1-49895-49738-7/7/2021

TABLE OF CONTENTS

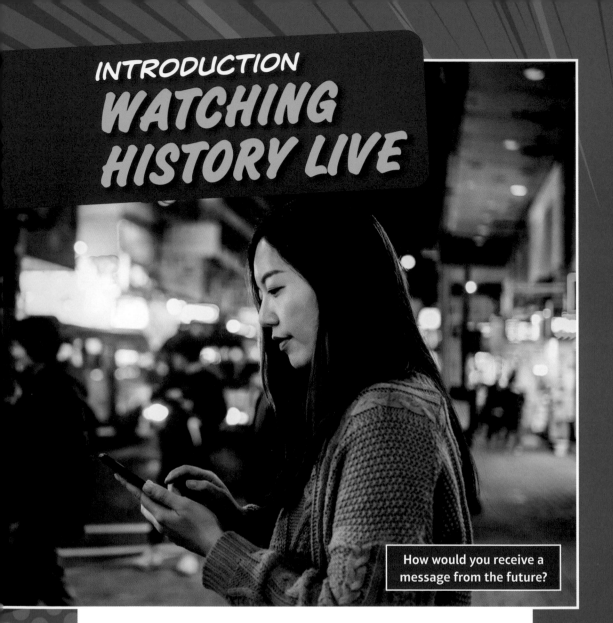

INTRODUCTION
WATCHING HISTORY LIVE

How would you receive a message from the future?

Alert! An important message was just sent your way. You have received a distress call—from the future! Good thing you have a special machine for just this purpose. It allows you to go to any day, at any time, in the future or in the past. You jump in your time machine and rush to the year 2070 to save your friend who is in danger.

Traveling through time is scary. But seeing what the world will be like in the future is a thrill. You open your eyes and look out the window. You see a city skyline in the distance. The buildings are just like the structures you've seen on science fiction shows. You've made it. Now it's time to help your friend.

Time travel has captured our imaginations for a long time. But humans have never built a real time machine. Is it even possible?

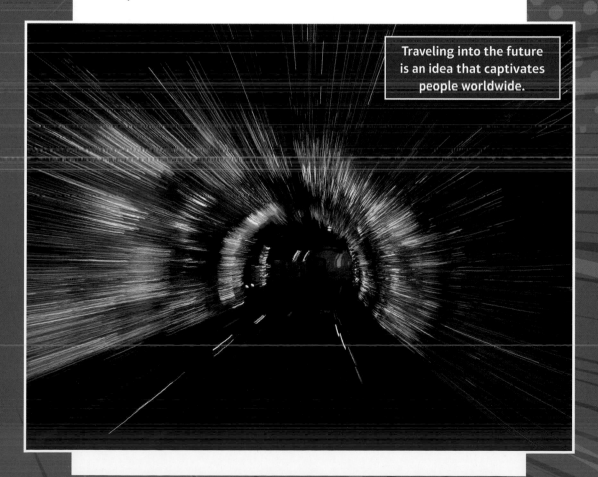

Traveling into the future is an idea that captivates people worldwide.

CHAPTER 1
TIME TRAVEL ACROSS STORIES

Traveling to the past to see dinosaurs in real life would be exciting and scary.

Fantasy and science fiction movies, books, and comics let us imagine what time travel could be like. Who wouldn't want to witness major events from the past? What if you could talk to people from other time periods? Are you curious about what life will be like in the future? If you had superpowers, you might be able to travel through time to see for yourself! The possibilities are exciting and endless.

Visiting a time other than the present has captured the imagination of writers, illustrators, and movie directors for a long time. The idea of time travel first appeared in a Hindu text from the ninth century BCE. It took a while for time travel to catch on, though. It didn't start appearing regularly in stories until the late nineteenth century.

Many people are fascinated by traveling back in time to correct mistakes or traveling forward in time to see what the future is like.

SUPERFAST FACT

Time is the only known dimension that allows us to move in only one direction.

Sometimes in stories, a strange-looking machine helps a time-jumping character travel. The machine might look like a flying car or a telephone booth. It could even look like a regular school bus! Other times, the time machine is smaller, or it is a stationary device, such as an hourglass or a treadmill.

Cars like this one can become time machines in movies and stories.

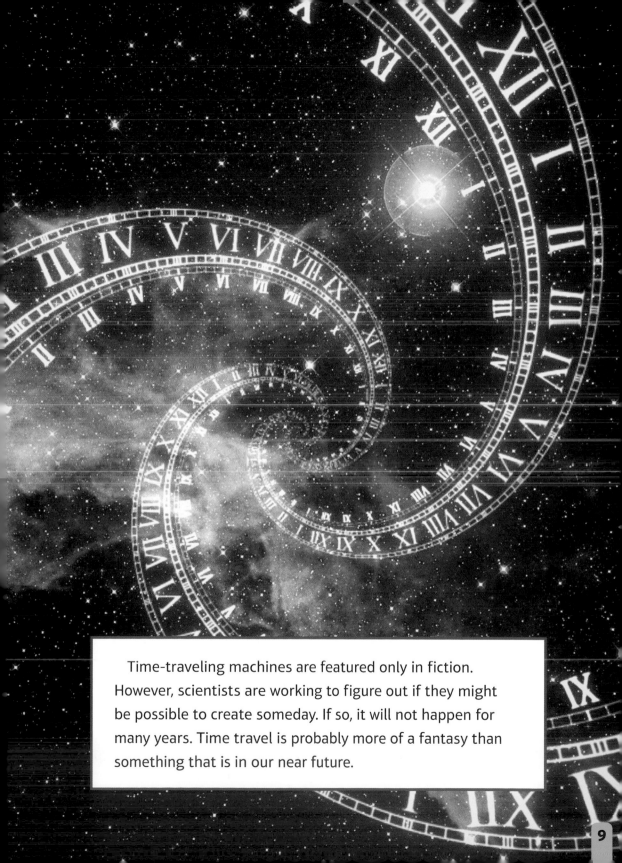

Time-traveling machines are featured only in fiction. However, scientists are working to figure out if they might be possible to create someday. If so, it will not happen for many years. Time travel is probably more of a fantasy than something that is in our near future.

CHAPTER 2
WHAT IS TIME TRAVEL, EXACTLY?

Light moves much faster than any object in the universe can move.

Light is the fastest thing in the universe. The speed of light in space is more than 186,000 miles (299,274 km) per second. But if someone could travel close to this speed, time would move more slowly for them.

Albert Einstein proved that time depends on your speed. Imagine two people moving at drastically different speeds. One person is traveling through space at ninety percent of the speed of light. The other person is walking normally on Earth. A span of twenty minutes for the walking person would only be ten minutes for the space traveler.

Some fictional heroes can move faster than the speed of light. They might disappear for a fraction of a second. In that time, they could travel across the globe to pick up a taco or stop a bad guy from committing a crime. To people moving more slowly, the characters appear to be traveling through time.

Einstein believed that space and time were part of a whole called space-time.

Physics is the scientific study of matter. Physicists study how matter moves, how it relates to energy, and particles. Particles are very small pieces of matter that make up everything in the universe. But there is more than one kind of particle. Elementary particles are the building blocks of other types of particles. There are two main types: fermions and bosons. Fermions make up all matter. Bosons are energy-carrying particles.

Light can behave like a wave or like a stream of particles.

Physicists identify four known dimensions in the universe—height, depth, width, and time. These dimensions make up space-time. Most modern physicists believe moving backward in time is impossible for people. But in 2019, scientists used a computer to simulate sending a particle back in time. The more particles that were added, the less successful the experiment was. But it was an important addition to time-travel theory.

Scientists use supercomputers to run time-travel experiments.

Physical time travel is still impossible. But we can travel through time in our minds. Mental time travel is the ability to imagine the past and the future. People who mentally time travel can remember specific events and apply them to the future. Mental time travel helps humans survive. For instance, farmers can think about techniques they've used in the past to grow crops. They imagine ways to improve those techniques in future growing seasons.

Babies are not born with this superskill. But by age five, most kids can imagine and talk about future events. These skills continue to improve into adulthood. However, as people age, their brains age as well. Their ability to mentally travel forward and backward in time gets harder.

Humans can think about future scenarios, allowing us to "travel" to the future in our imaginations.

AMAZING ANIMAL POWER

For a long time, scientists believed only humans could mentally time travel. But many are rethinking that idea. Birds called scrub jays hide food for later. They can imagine a future when they will want to eat the food they hid. Bird migration might be another example of mental time travel. From past experience, birds know winter will get cold, so they leave before the weather changes. They imagine a future with colder days and take actions to avoid them.

Some birds hide food to eat later.

CHAPTER 3
OTHER TIME TRAVEL POSSIBILITIES

You can spin a globe two ways, but Earth only spins from west to east.

Some fantasy characters can run or fly so fast that their motion causes Earth to spin the other way. In movies and science fiction stories, this change in rotation reverses time too. To make Earth spin backward, a character would need to fly at nearly the speed of light. The hero would also need to be millions of times more massive than Earth to have the force to push the planet.

Causing Earth to spin in the opposite direction wouldn't really reverse time. But physicists and scientists are working hard to figure out other ways in which time travel could be a real possibility in the future. They have many different theories.

The top of Mount Everest is the highest place on Earth. Time moves differently there than it does at lower elevations.

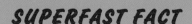

SUPERFAST FACT

Time goes faster at high altitudes than at sea level. It is a tiny difference, but it's there!

Astronomer Frank Tipler had an idea for an infinitely long cylinder made of dense matter. The Tipler Cylinder would spin at nearly the speed of light. If you traveled around the cylinder in one direction, you'd travel forward in time. If you went the opposite way, you'd travel backward in time. But building an infinitely long cylinder would be impossible. And the cylinder, no matter what the length, would probably crush the time traveler. Like Earth, its mass would pull the traveler toward its surface. Then the traveler would be squashed by gravity.

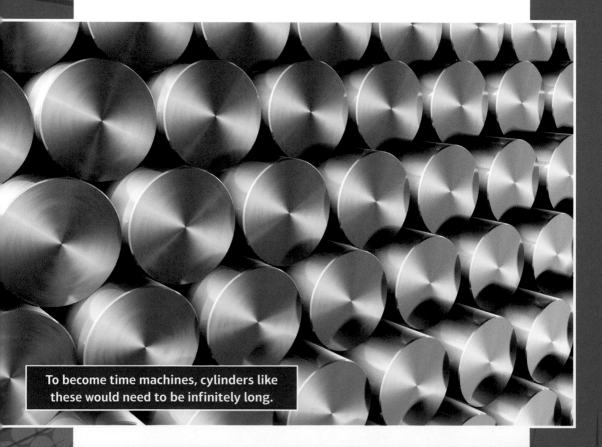

To become time machines, cylinders like these would need to be infinitely long.

Astronomer Frank Tipler has unique ideas about how time travel might work.

Physicist Stephen Hawking had a time-travel idea that involved black holes. A spaceship would spin around a black hole. The rotation and gravity of the black hole would make the ship accelerate to nearly the speed of light. The people on the spaceship would experience half the time experienced by people not near the black hole. If they circled the black hole for five years, ten years would pass elsewhere!

Black holes have such strong gravity that even light can't escape from them.

No one knows for sure if cosmic strings exist.

Cosmic strings are the source of another time travel theory. When the universe began, cracks in space-time known as cosmic strings might have formed. Cosmic strings are narrow tubes of energy that stretch across the universe.

Two cosmic strings parallel to each other would bend space-time. Astronauts in a spaceship that traveled along the path of a bend would experience time differently than people outside the ship.

CHAPTER 4

CONTROLLING THE FUTURE

Wormholes are hypothetical. Scientists have many theories about them but are unable to prove their existence.

Wormholes are shortcuts between two points in space. Some scientists believe that wormholes are all around us. They are just too small to see. Wormholes could be made up of two black holes connected by a passage. With a wormhole, you could travel between two places in a short amount of time. No one has discovered a real wormhole yet. But some scientists think they could play a part in time travel.

It is thought that time machines would need matter with negative energy density to travel through wormholes. Gravity pulls objects made of normal matter together. But objects with negative energy density would push away from one another. Unfortunately, negative energy density is still just an idea.

Some science fiction stories depict people traveling through artificial wormholes.

SUPERFAST FACT

Wormholes are probably so small that only tiny things could travel through them. And their extreme gravity would crush anything inside.

Space-time around a black hole could be warped into a doughnut shape by gravity.

Wormholes are unlikely to be a real option for time travel. But what about doughnut holes? Some scientists believe that parts of space could be twisted into a doughnut shape. This would create a gravity field that curves space-time into a loop. The hole in the middle would be a black hole. To travel back in time, a traveler would race around inside the doughnut. They would go back further into the past with each loop.

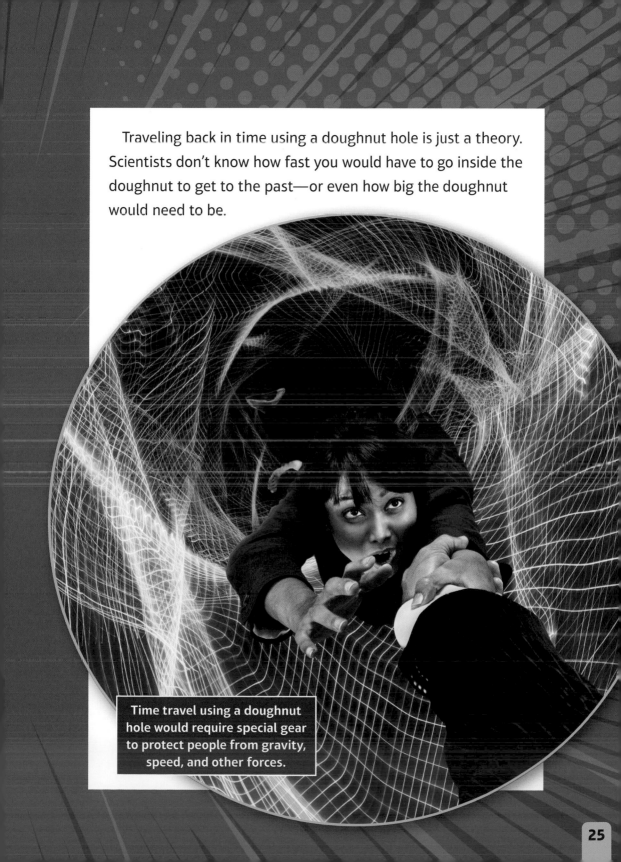

Traveling back in time using a doughnut hole is just a theory. Scientists don't know how fast you would have to go inside the doughnut to get to the past—or even how big the doughnut would need to be.

Time travel using a doughnut hole would require special gear to protect people from gravity, speed, and other forces.

Time travel comes with some unique ethical questions. If you could travel back in time, would you try to stop a person from doing something that you consider wrong? What would happen if you met yourself in the past? Could you accidentally stop yourself from being born?

One theory in many movies and TV shows is the butterfly effect. If you went back in time and took a simple action, such as crossing a street, could it affect everything in the future? The butterfly effect says that a simple action, such as a butterfly flapping its wings, can set off a chain of events that would alter reality.

Scientists say the butterfly effect probably doesn't exist. They have no way to prove that such minor occurrences can cause larger, unrelated consequences.

The butterfly effect explores how small, seemingly unimportant actions can alter the future.

The universe has billions of galaxies.

SUPER STEM BREAKTHROUGH

Astronomers used a giant radio telescope in Chile to study a galaxy called ALESS 073.1 that formed more than 12 billion years ago. The light from the galaxy took billions of years to reach the telescope because the galaxy is so far away. This allowed astronomers to see the galaxy as it was billions of years ago.

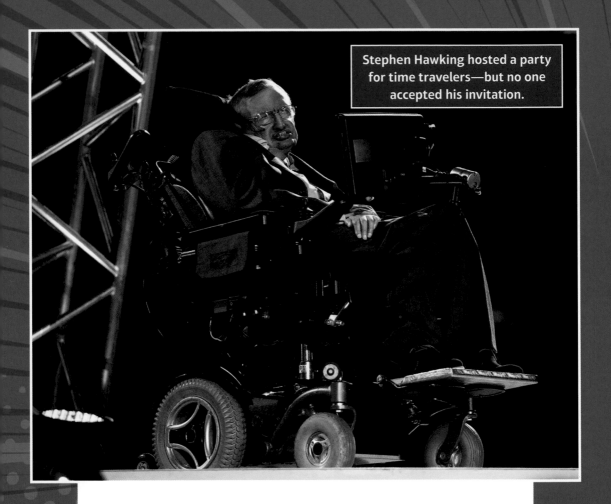

Stephen Hawking hosted a party for time travelers—but no one accepted his invitation.

In 2009, Stephen Hawking came up with an idea to settle the time travel debate once and for all. He threw a party, but he didn't send out invitations until after the party ended. If a time traveler received the invitation, that person would be able to travel back in time to attend the party. But no one did.

Time travel is still just an idea. Until we figure out its mysteries, we can watch our favorite characters defy the laws of space-time in books, movies, and TV shows. Someday, it may be more than a theory. Then you will be able to time travel too.

SUPER YOU!

Can you imagine what the world will look like in one hundred years? Mentally time travel to the future and draw pictures of what you see. What will homes be like in the future? How will people travel? How will phones and computers change?

GLOSSARY

altitude: height above sea level

black hole: an object in space with gravity so strong that light cannot escape it

cosmic string: a hypothetical object in space that is very long and thin and formed early in the universe

matter: something that occupies space and has mass

particle: a very small piece of matter; everything in our universe is made of particles

physics: the study of matter

space-time: a system of one time and three spatial dimensions by which any physical object or event can be located

speed of light: the speed at which light travels in space

theory: a general rule offered to explain something in science

wormhole: a hypothetical structure in space seen as a tunnel connecting two points

LEARN MORE

Armstrong, Neil. *Bok's Giant Leap: One Moon Rock's Journey through Time and Space.* New York: Crown Books for Young Readers, 2021.

DeCristofano, Carolyn Cinami. *A Black Hole Is Not a Hole: Updated and Expanded Edition.* Watertown, MA: Charlesbridge, 2021.

Doeden, Matt. *Stephen Hawking: Celebrated Physicist.* Minneapolis: Lerner Publications, 2021.

Kiddle: Time Travel Facts for Kids
https://kids.kiddle.co/Time_travel

Mara, Wil. *Albert Einstein.* New York: Dorling Kindersley, 2019.

NASA: Is Time Travel Possible?
https://spaceplace.nasa.gov/time-travel/en/

Our Universe for Kids: Time Travel
https://www.ouruniverseforkids.com/time-travel/

Science Kids: Is Time Travel Possible?
https://www.sciencekids.co.nz/videos/physics/timetravel.html

INDEX

Photo Acknowledgments

Image credits: d3sign/Getty Images, p.4; Terraxplorer/Getty Images, p.5; JoeLena/Getty Images, p.6; Loren Zemlicka/Getty Images, p.7; Grzegorz Czapski/ Shutterstock, p.8; lashMovie/Shutterstock, p.9; Yiu Yu Hoi/Getty Images, p.10; Keystone/Stringer/Getty Images, p.11; Yuichiro Chino/Getty Images, p.12; Kyodo/Newscom, p.13; SDI Productions/Getty Images, p.14; Moelyn Photos/ Getty Images, p.15; Buena Vista Images/Getty Images, p.16; Nicole Kucera/Getty Images, p.17; sitox/Getty Images, p.18; Campus Party Italia/flckr.com, p.19; MARK GARLICK/SCIENCE PHOTO LIBRARY/Getty Images, p.20; NeoLeo/Shutterstock, p.21; KTSDESIGN/SCIENCE PHOTO LIBRARY/Getty Images, p.22; Colin Anderson Productions pty ltd/Getty Images, 23; MARK GARLICK/SCIENCE PHOTO LIBRARY/ Getty Images, p.24; John M Lund Photography Inc/Getty Images, p.25; Gregoria Gregoriou Crowe fine art and creative photography/Getty Images, p.26; Handout/ Getty Images, p.27; Dan Kitwood/Staff/Getty Images, p.28; Pavel_Chag/Getty Images, p.29;

Cover: mikkelwilliam/Getty Images